Contents

Some words are shown in bold, **like this.** You can find out what they mean by looking in the glossary.

Which mole's nose is its star attraction?

In this book you will meet a lizard that can squirt blood from its eyes. You will also learn about strange plants that eat animals. Being weird can be wonderful.

In certain kinds of soil, a star-nosed mole can dig a 4.5-metre tunnel in an hour.

Meet the star-nosed mole

The star-nosed mole has a sniffer that looks like a many-pointed star. Twenty-two fleshy bits of skin form a circle around its nose.

The star-nosed mole is a type of **mammal** known as an insectivore, or insect eater. It lives in damp forests and marshy areas in eastern North America.

This mole has unusually large front feet. It uses them to dig underground tunnels where it lives. It also uses them to paddle through water, where it finds fish and water insects to eat.

Did you know?

The star-nosed mole can swim very well. It can even swim under ice.

What's up with that nose?

The star-nosed mole really needs its nose, but not for smelling. It has a poor sense of smell, and it is almost blind. You might be wondering how it survives at all.

Its weird nose is the **adaptation** that saves the day. It has 22 **tentacles** that are very sensitive. They give the star-nosed mole one of the best senses of touch in the animal kingdom.

The star has about 100,000 nerve fibres in it. These fibres carry messages to the brain about what the mole touches. It also helps the mole sense the slightest movement by **prey** such as earthworms and insects.

The star on the star-nosed mole is a little more than 1 centimetre across.

Which mammal can lick a whole army of ants?

The giant anteater can eat 30,000 ants or termites a day. Yet it has no teeth. Instead, it has an amazing 60-centimetre-long tongue. It can snap its tongue in and out of an anthill 150 times per minute.

The female giant anteater carries her baby on her back until it is about a year old.

The giant anteater is a **mammal** about the size of an Alsatian dog. It lives in forests and grasslands in Central and South America. Its head is long and narrow with a tube-like snout.

The giant anteater shuffles slowly along on the sides of its front feet to keep its long sharp claws from getting worn down. But giant anteaters can be quick sometimes. If a jaguar attacks, the anteater will rear up and slash at its enemy with its claws.

How to eat ants

All these strange things are **adaptations** that help the anteater survive. The nose at the end of its snout sniffs out **prey.** Its claws help it tear open the nest. Then it sticks its snout deep into the nest and flicks its tongue in and out. Ants stick to the gluey saliva on the tongue and the anteater slurps them up.

A giant anteater may eat only about 140 ants from any one nest at a time.

Ants fight back when an anteater tongue barges into their home. They swarm out and try to bite the anteater. But stiff hairs on the anteater's body help protect it from ant bites. Even so, the anteater usually leaves an anthill after a few minutes. It does not completely destroy it. It may want to eat there again. Instead of pigging out at one nest, the anteater visits many nests in a day.

Which birds have an eye for detail?

A male bowerbird tries to impress a female by building her a fancy place to **mate**. This sort of place is called a bower. He decorates the bower with feathers, berries, shells or mushrooms.

Some scientists think that showy bowerbirds like this golden bowerbird do not make their bowers as fancy as those made by plainer-looking bowerbirds.

Maypoles, mats and avenues

The **rainforests** of Australia and New Guinea are home to 17 **species** of bowerbirds. The type of bower a male bowerbird builds depends on his species. Some species are mat builders. They collect and arrange a layer of leaves on the forest floor, then decorate this mat with shells and other objects. One mat builder, the stagemaker, places silvery leaves around the edge of the mat. When the leaves dry out, he puts down new ones.

The male golden bowerbird is known for building maypole bowers. He sets up a tower of twigs around a small tree. Sometimes he makes more than one tower and builds bridges between them.

Some maypole builders also pluck moss from the forest floor. They replant it near the bower to make a little 'lawn'. Others collect flower blossoms to make a 'garden'. Some bowers are large enough for a child to sit in.

The Vogelkop bowerbird places thousands of objects on the 'lawn' in front of his bower. One bird even took a pair of green socks from scientists camped nearby!

Robot bowerbirds

Scientists turned some female bowerbird robots loose on real male bowerbirds. The males were easily fooled! Many of them tried to mate with the robots. Scientists filmed what happened, and will study the tapes to learn more about the mating habits of bowerbirds.

Other bowerbirds build an avenue, or street, for themselves. The male satin bowerbird sets up two walls of twigs with a little path between them. He then makes paint out of crushed plants, such as berries. Using a leaf or a small stick, he paints the inside of the bower.

But that is not all! He collects feathers, berries and other things that catch his eye. Coins and pieces of glass have ended up in bowers from time to time. One bowerbird even topped off his bower with a glass eye he found!

Getting the girl

Once a male bowerbird has finished his bower, he struts around and sings to attract females. His aim is to get one into the bower so they can **mate.**

A bower is not a nest. But if a female enters a male's bower and mates with him, she will build a nest nearby.

Did you know?

Satin bowerbirds usually decorate with blue items that match their own blue feathers.

Which bird can dance on water?

The western grebe is a wonderful dancer — as long as its dance floor is made of water. The western grebe of North America lives on lakes and marshes. It eats insects and fish, which it stabs with its long, pointed beak.

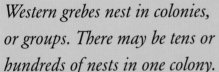

Western grebes nest in colonies, or groups. There may be tens or hundreds of nests in one colony.

Walking on land is hard for the western grebe. Its feet are so far back on its body, that it often tips over. Not surprisingly, it stays away from land. Even the nests that it builds float on water.

Flash paddling

Western grebes are known for the fancy dancing they do when they mate. A male and a female pair off and lift their bodies straight out of the water. Then they run, side by side, along the surface. They paddle their feet wildly to stay on top of the water. This is called the rushing display.

Which lizard sees (blood) red?

A horned lizard looks like a spiny, squashed toad. If the way it looks does not keep a **predator** away, the horned lizard can puff itself up and squirt a jet of blood at its enemy. That usually does the trick!

Desert life
The horned lizard is a **reptile.** It lives in hot, dry, sandy areas of western North America. It spends much of the day eating ants – its favourite food.

Horned lizards are sometimes mistakenly called 'horned toads' because they look a lot like toads.

The horned lizard looks scary. But most animals (except for ants) have nothing to fear from it. The horned lizard, however, has a few things to worry about. To coyotes, snakes and hawks, the horned lizard looks like dinner. Luckily, the horned lizard's colouring and markings **camouflage** it. It can also burrow into the sand.

Getting back at the enemy

Some predators find and catch the horned lizard anyway. When this happens, the lizard puffs itself up with air. It ends up looking like a balloon with horns and spikes. These horns and spikes can be deadly. Snakes and birds that try to eat them will probably die. As they swallow, the lizard's horns tear through their throat.

The spiky balloon trick does not always work. If it fails, the horned lizard has another defence. It increases the blood pressure in its head until blood jets out from the corners of its eyes. Scientists think that the blood probably tastes bad. After being squirted with blood, the predator usually drops the lizard and tries to get the bad taste out of its mouth.

A horned lizard can squirt blood a distance of about 1 metre. It may put as much as one-third of the blood in its body into the effort.

Which reptile is a living fossil?

Over long periods of time, most animal **species** change. They change in small ways so that they are better able to survive. But the tuatara has hardly changed at all in 200 million years! Back then, the dinosaurs were still alive.

The word tuatara *means 'spiny back' in Maori. Maori is the language spoken by the native peoples of New Zealand.*

Meet the tuatara

The tuatara is a **reptile** that looks like a lizard. But it is not closely related to lizards. Its skeleton, teeth and **mating** habits are all very different from those of lizards. All the tuatara's closest relatives became **extinct** at the same time as the dinosaurs.

The tuatara lives only on islands off the coast of New Zealand. It often shares a burrow with a seabird. At night, the tuatara searches for insects, snails and birds' eggs to eat. Although it has legs, it sprawls along the ground rather like a snake, with its belly scraping the earth.

Did you know?

Tuataras do not mate until they are between 10 and 20 years old. Scientists think they may live to be more than 100 years old.

An extra eye

The tuatara has a third eye. This eye can be seen through the skin on the top of a baby tuatara's head. The eye can only tell the difference between light and dark.

The tuatara has a few **predators** such as hawks and seagulls. But rats that are not **native** to the islands are its biggest enemy. Rats eat tuatara eggs and babies. Scientists are working to get rid of the rats. They also breed tuataras and release them on rat-free islands.

This tuatara is eating a weta, an insect that also lives only in New Zealand. Wetas are large, up to 2.5 centimetres long.

Which frog likes to hang out in termite nests?

Most frogs live near streams and ponds. Not the turtle frog. Because its favourite food is termites, it can often be found living right inside an underground termite nest.

If you were to pick up the turtle frog, it would feel like a floppy, half-empty water balloon.

Meet the turtle frog

The turtle frog is an **amphibian** that lives in dry, sandy areas of western Australia. Its wide, flat body and short stubby legs make it look more like a turtle than a frog. It does not act much like a frog, either. The turtle frog spends most of its time underground and almost never goes near water. Its stumpy legs are **adaptations** for this underground life. It uses them to dig burrows or to dig down into a termite nest.

Many **species** of frogs lay eggs in water. Tadpoles hatch from the eggs and slowly develop into adult frogs. But the female turtle frog lays eggs in wet sand. The tadpole stage is completed inside the eggs. When the eggs hatch, the babies are fully formed frogs.

Gastric-brooding frogs

When the female gastric-brooding frog of Australia has laid her eggs, she swallows them. The eggs develop in her stomach. When the female is ready to 'give birth', the baby frogs crawl up out of her stomach and pop out of her mouth! Gastric-brooding frogs have not been seen in the wild since the early 1980s. They are now thought to be **extinct.**

Which fish have their own fishing rods?

An anglerfish uses its own built-in 'fishing rod' to go fishing. The fishing rod on top of an anglerfish's head is a long fin with a bit of flesh dangling from it. This fleshy **lure** may have markings that look like eyes, fins and scales. Fish that go for the lure probably think that they have just found their supper. Instead they end up being eaten by the anglerfish.

Non-swimmers

There are about **210 species** of anglerfish. All have some type of rod and lure. And all look lumpy, spiny and odd. Most live near the bottom of the sea and are not very good swimmers. Instead of swimming, some pull themselves along the bottom using their **pectoral fins**.

*An anglerfish's fishing rod is actually part of its **dorsal fin**.*

Light-up lures and stretchy stomachs

Anglerfish have other **adaptations** that help them catch **prey.** In many species, the lure lights up. Because sunlight does not reach the bottom of the sea, it is pitch black there. The shining lure helps attract prey. Anglerfish also have very stretchy stomachs. An anglerfish can eat a fish larger than itself.

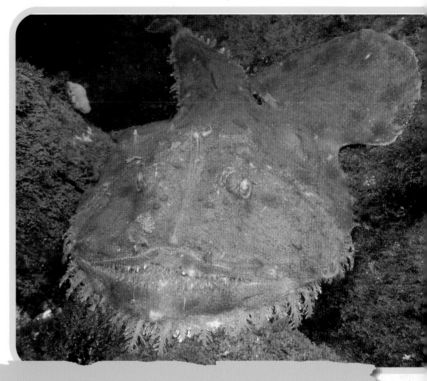

The goosefish is an anglerfish that sometimes lives in shallow waters. It usually just catches fish, but when it is closer to the surface it will eat seabirds.

Bioluminescence

In the dark depths of the sea, many animals make their own light. This is known as bioluminescence. Animals may use it to help them see better, to lure prey, or to scare off **predators.** Light is produced when special chemicals mix inside an animal's body. In the anglerfish, the glow is produced by chemical reactions inside **bacteria** that live in an anglerfish's lure.

The female is the fisher

In some **species** of anglerfish, the male is practically useless. He is much smaller than the female and has no rod or **lure**. This makes it hard for him to find food on his own. To solve the problem, he becomes a **parasite.** The male bites his female **mate,** and his jaws become permanently attached to her body.

The male anglerfish finds a female by sensing a chemical that she releases. You might say she smells nice and fishy to him.

Soon the bloodstreams of the two fish join. **Nutrients** from the food that the female eats feed both fish. Eventually, the male's body wastes away. Well, at least the female never has to search for her mate!

Which fish is all mouth?

The gulper eel's mouth takes up about half of its body, which might be 0.6 to1.8 metres long. It has no problem eating a fish almost as big as itself.

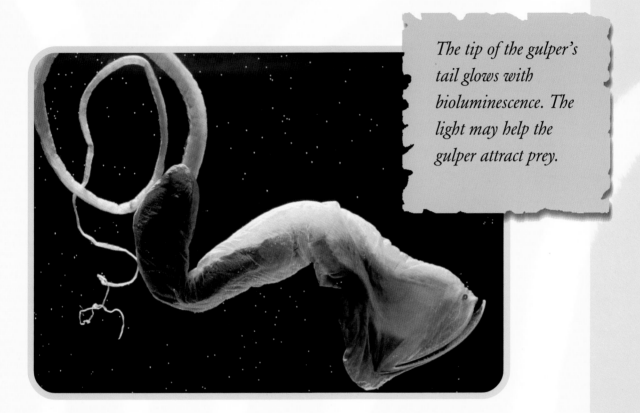

The tip of the gulper's tail glows with bioluminescence. The light may help the gulper attract prey.

The gulper eel is a fish. It lives at depths of 1980 metres or more, where it is always dark. Food is very scarce in this part of the sea. To deal with such a harsh **habitat,** the gulper eel has several **adaptations.**

Its body is simple. It is basically just a giant mouth attached to a giant stomach, finished off with a long thin tail. If a large fish swims past, the gulper eel can unhinge its jaws to make its mouth even bigger. It might be a long time before the eel gets another chance to eat.

Which molluscs are bizarre but beautiful?

The Spanish dancer sea slug spreads its 'wings' to swim away from danger. It can grow as long as 50 centimetres.

Sea slugs come in a wonderful variety of colours, patterns and shapes. Sea slugs are **molluscs** that live in the sea. Most crawl along the seabed, but some swim or float.

Slugs pack a punch

Most sea slugs eat simple water creatures like corals and sponges. But the blue sea slugs eat a poisonous sea creature known as the Portuguese man-of-war. When the sea slugs eat these creatures, they store the poison in feathery body parts called cerata. These cerata become extremely poisonous. Even though blue sea slugs can be only about 4 centimetres long, they can give a painful sting. This is one way in which blue sea slugs protect themselves.

Blue sea slugs also protect themselves by floating upside down. This puts their white and blue bottoms on top and helps them blend in with the blue of the seawater. **Predators,** such as seabirds, gliding above the water have trouble seeing them. Their topsides, which are now on the bottom, are grey. This makes them less visible to predators below them. This type of **protective colouration** is known as countershading.

Blue slugs like this one have a gas bubble in their stomachs that helps them float.

Sea slug food factories

Some **species** of sea slugs eat algae, a simple lifeform that carries out **photosynthesis.** The sea slugs **digest** all of the algae except the chloroplasts, which are where photosynthesis takes place. The chloroplasts continue to carry out photosynthesis inside a slug's body. The slugs still eat small sea animals, but they can also get food the same way a plant does.

Which beetle can bring itself to the boil?

A bombardier is a soldier who drops bombs. The bombardier beetle is called after this type of soldier because it can turn itself into a mini bomber!

The bombardier beetle can blast a predator coming from any direction.

Boiling point

The inside of a bombardier beetle is like a mad scientist's lab. When a **predator** is near, chemicals inside the beetle's body start mixing together and heating up. The beetle squirts the boiling-hot liquid out of its backside with a loud pop, and a poisonous steam cloud rolls straight at its enemy. This 'bomb' can kill small insects.

Usually, the bombardier beetle leads a peaceful life. It spends its days under rocks or dead leaves. At night it hunts for insects and slugs. But it doesn't bomb them. It just grabs them and chews them up.

Which plants are deathtraps?

You don't think of plants as being killers. But carnivorous plants attract, catch, kill and **digest** animals! They are carnivores just like lions and tigers. But carnivorous plants eat much smaller **prey**, such as insects and spiders. About 600 **species** of carnivorous plants have been discovered. However, some have become **extinct.**

Carnivorous plants grow in or near bogs and swamps in most parts of the world. The water washes away the **nutrient** nitrogen that plants need to grow. So carnivorous plants get their nitrogen from insects and other small animals.

Sundews

Sundews have 'traps' to catch prey. The Venus flytrap is a sundew native to North and South Carolina, USA. After catching three or four insects, a venus flytrap leaf dies.

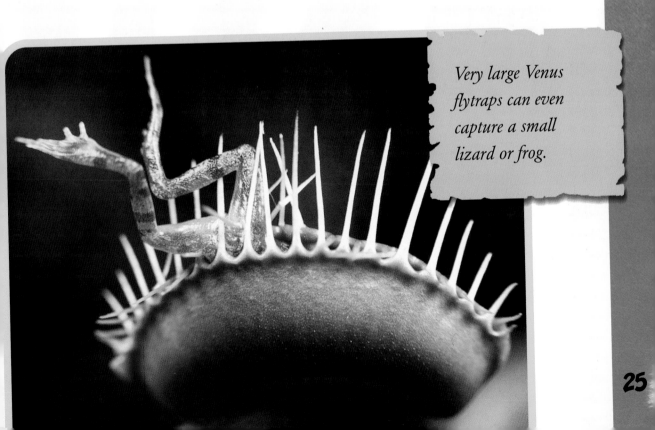

Very large Venus flytraps can even capture a small lizard or frog.

Catching dinner

A structure like a hinge runs down the middle of each round leaf. Insects are attracted to a sticky liquid on the leaves. When an insect brushes against hairs on a leaf, the leaf folds inwards quickly. The insect is trapped inside. The plant then produces a juice that **digests** the insect in about ten days.

Other types of sundew lure insects with sticky drops of liquid that cling to hairlike growths on their leaves. If an insect touches this gluey liquid, it gets stuck. It cannot work itself free, and juice from the plant flows over it. The juice dissolves the insect into a liquid that the plant then digests.

The sticky liquid on the leaves glistens in the sun like dew.

Pitcher plants

Pitcher plants have tube-shaped leaves that look like vases, trumpets or small pitchers. The lip of the 'pitcher' is covered with **nectar.**

Once an insect touches the nectar, it slides down the slippery insides of the pitcher and plops into some liquid at the bottom. The insect usually cannot climb out. It drowns in the bottom of the pitcher and the plant digests it.

This pitcher plant grows on the island of Borneo in Malaysia.

The cobra plant

The cobra plant of Oregon and California, USA looks like a snake that is ready to strike. It even has a long purplish 'tongue'. Nectar on this tongue attracts insects. Once inside the plant, the insect tries to fly out through 'windows' that look like openings. Soon the insect gets worn out trying to escape. It falls into a puddle of liquid at the bottom of the plant. **Bacteria** living in the plant break down the insect for the plant.

☑ The Mount Lyell salamander lives under rocks on mountainsides. If a **predator** lifts a rock and finds the salamander, the salamander curls into a ball and rolls down the mountain and away from the predator.

☑ A species of marsupial frog in South America can carry as many as 100 eggs in a pouch on her back. The eggs develop into tadpoles in the pouch, then the female releases them into a stream.

☑ The male giraffe-necked weevil looks as if it has a very long neck. The neck is actually a snout with a set of jaws at the end. Some giraffe-necked weevils can be 5 to 8 centimetres long, most of which is their long snout.

The giraffe-necked weevil is a kind of beetle.

☑ The olm is a type of salamander that lives in caves. Its eyes are covered with skin and it is a white-pink colour. Olms are so strange-looking that in 1859 the scientist Charles Darwin called them 'wrecks of ancient life'.

Snake-necked turtles have necks that are sometimes as long as their shells. When a snakeneck turtle is ready to eat, it rapidly straightens its neck and grabs its **prey.** It pulls its head back by bending its neck sideways under the edge of its shell.

This snake-necked turtle extends its long neck.

There is a frog in South America that gets smaller as it gets older. During the tadpole stage, it can reach 25 centimetres in length. As an adult frog it is only about 5 centimetres long.

The mole lizard of Mexico looks like a pale pink worm. It has a tiny pair of front legs but no back legs. To get around it pulls itself forward with its two little front legs.

Glossary

adaptation   special feature that helps a plant or animal survive

amphibian   animal that lives part of its life in water and part of its life on land

bacteria   very tiny lifeforms that can only be seen with a microscope

camouflage   change the way something looks so it will not be so easy to see

digest   break down food so it can be absorbed in the stomach

dorsal fin   fin on the back of a fish and some marine animals

extinct   no longer living on Earth

habitat   place where an animal lives in the wild

lure   a type of bait used in fishing

mammal   animal that is warm-blooded, has hair or fur, a backbone and drinks milk made by its mother

mate   partner with whom an animal makes babies; also the pairing of a male and female so they can have babies

mollusc   soft-bodied animal that has no bones

native   plants or animals that have always lived in a particular area

nectar   sweet liquid made by plants and used to attract insects and birds

nutrient   food substance that a plant or animal needs to survive

parasite   animal or plant that gets its food by living on or in another animal or plant

pectoral fin   one of a pair of fins located on the side of a fish's body just behind the head

photosynthesis   process in which energy from sunlight is used to change carbon dioxide gas and water into food. Green plants, algae and some bacteria carry out photosynthesis.

predator   animal that hunts, kills and eats another type of animal

prey   animal that is hunted by other animals for food

protective colouration   colours or markings on an animal's body that help it blend in with its surroundings so predators will be unable to see it

rainforest   thick forest of tall trees where it rains almost every day

reptile   cold-blooded animal with scaly skin and a backbone that breathes through lungs

species group of animals that have the same features and can have babies with each other

tentacle long thin body part on an animal's head or near its mouth that it uses to sense its surroundings

More books to read

Amazing Nature: Clever Camouflage, John Woodward
(Heinemann Library, 2004)

Amazing Nature: Dramatic Displays, Tim Knight
(Heinemann Library, 2004)

Animal Encyclopedia:
(Dorling Kindersley Publishers, 2000)

From Egg to Adult: The Life Cycle of Amphibians, Mike Unwin
(Heinemann Library, 2003)

Go Facts: Reptiles, Paul McEvoy
(A & C Black, 2003)

Life in a Cave, Clare Oliver
(Franklin Watts, 2002)

The Variety of Life: Molluscs, Joy Richardson
(Franklin Watts, 2003)

Index